Once upon a time, in the small town of Riviera, there was a joyful and curious little girl named Lina.

She loved spending her time exploring the world, but one particular day was about to change her life forever.

One sunny afternoon, Lina went to a fair with her parents.

At the turn of an alley, she discovered a miniature karting stand. The tiny race cars zipped around a winding track at full speed.

Lina's eyes lit up with fascination. She was captivated by the frenetic energy of the karts and the roar of the engines. It was as if a spark had ignited within her. In that moment, Lina had a revelation: she wanted to become a karting driver.

Lina discovered that karting was more than just a race. It was a blend of adrenaline, friendship, and exciting challenges. Over the weeks, she proved to be a talented and determined driver.

Finally, the day of the big Riviera karting championship arrived. Lina stood on the starting line, her heart racing. Her parents and new friends were there to support her. When the light turned green, she launched on to the track.

The race was intense, featuring tight turns and high-speed straights. Lina showed great courage and strategy, overtaking her competitors with impressive skill. By the end of the day, she crossed the finish line in first place, to the cheers of the crowd.

www.ingramcontent.com/pod-product-compliance
Lightning Source LLC
Chambersburg PA
CBHW041403010526
44107CB00015B/1058